Embroidery Mastery
Unveiling the Quilting Artistry through 4 Distinctive Stitches Book

Killian A Yarnell

THIS BOOK
BELONGS TO

....

....

With so many books out there to choose from, I want to thank you for choosing this one and taking precious time out of your life to buy and read my work. Readers like you are the reason I take such passion in creating these books.

It is with gratitude and humility that I express how honored I am to become a part of your life and I hope that you take the same pleasure in reading this book as I did in writing it.

Can I ask one small favour? I ask that you write an honest and open review on Amazon of what you thought of the book. This will help other readers make an informed choice on whether to buy this book.

My sincerest thanks.

Table of Contents

SUMMARY	1
CHAPTER 1 - Introduction	24
CHAPTER 2 - Fabric Preparation, Cutting, and Painting	30
CHAPTER 3 - Sewing	46
CHAPTER 4 - Making and Basting the Quilt Sandwich	51
CHAPTER 5 - Embroidery	56
CHAPTER 6 - Quilting and Designing	75
CHAPTER 7 - Finishing Off	93

SUMMARY

Introduction to Quilting on the Couch:

Quilting on the Couch is a popular and enjoyable hobby that allows individuals to create beautiful and functional pieces of art from fabric. This activity can be done from the comfort of your own home, making it a convenient and relaxing pastime. Whether you are a beginner or an experienced quilter, quilting on the couch offers a creative outlet that can be both rewarding and therapeutic.

Quilting is the process of sewing together layers of fabric to create a quilt. Traditionally, quilts were made for practical purposes, such as providing warmth and comfort. However, quilting has evolved into a form of artistic expression, with quilters using various techniques and designs to create visually stunning pieces. Quilts can be made in a variety of sizes, from small wall hangings to large bedspreads, and can be customized to suit individual preferences and styles.

One of the advantages of quilting on the couch is the convenience it offers. Unlike other crafts that require a dedicated workspace or specialized equipment, quilting can be done on a couch or any comfortable seating area. All you need is a sewing machine, fabric, and basic quilting supplies such as scissors, pins, and a cutting mat. This accessibility makes quilting on the couch a great option for those who may not have a dedicated craft room or who prefer to work in a more relaxed environment.

Another benefit of quilting on the couch is the opportunity for relaxation and stress relief. Many people find the repetitive nature of quilting to be soothing and calming. The rhythmic motion of sewing and the focus required to piece together fabric can help to quiet the mind and promote a sense of mindfulness. Quilting on the couch can be a form of self-care, allowing individuals to unwind and recharge after a long day.

Quilting on the couch also provides a creative outlet for individuals to express their personal style and artistic vision. With countless fabric options available, quilters can choose from a wide range of colors, patterns, and textures to create unique and one-of-a-kind quilts. Additionally, quilting techniques such as appliqué, patchwork, and free-motion quilting allow for endless possibilities in design. Quilting on the couch allows individuals to explore their creativity and create pieces that reflect their own personal taste and aesthetic.

In conclusion, quilting on the couch is a versatile and enjoyable hobby that offers numerous benefits. From the convenience of being able to quilt from the comfort of your

Rediscovering the Joy of Hand Quilting:

A Journey Back to Tradition and Creativity

In today's fast-paced and technology-driven world, it's easy to overlook the simple pleasures and satisfaction that can be found in traditional crafts. Hand quilting, once a common practice passed down through generations, has become somewhat of a lost art. However, there is a growing movement of individuals who are rediscovering the joy of hand quilting and embracing it as a way to reconnect with their creativity and heritage.

Hand quilting is a process that involves stitching together layers of fabric to create a quilt. Unlike machine quilting, which is done using a sewing machine, hand quilting requires patience, precision, and a deep appreciation for the art form. Each stitch is carefully placed, creating intricate patterns and designs that can't be replicated by a machine.

One of the reasons why hand quilting is experiencing a resurgence in popularity is the sense of connection it provides to the past. Many quilters today are drawn to the craft because it allows them to honor their ancestors and carry on a tradition that has been passed down through generations. By working with their hands and using techniques that have been used for centuries, quilters feel a sense of continuity and a connection to those who came before them.

Another reason why hand quilting is gaining traction is the therapeutic and meditative nature of the craft. In a world filled with constant distractions and digital overload, hand quilting offers a respite from the chaos. The repetitive motion of stitching, the feel of the fabric, and the focus required to create intricate designs all contribute to a sense of calm and mindfulness. Many quilters find that the act of quilting allows them to slow down, be present in the moment, and find solace in the creative process.

Hand quilting also offers a level of creativity and artistic expression that can't be achieved through machine quilting. With hand quilting, quilters have complete control over every stitch and can experiment with different patterns, colors, and textures. This freedom allows for a truly unique and personalized quilt that reflects the quilter's individual style and vision. The satisfaction of seeing a quilt come together, stitch by stitch, is unparalleled and can't be replicated by simply pressing a button on a sewing machine.

Furthermore, hand quilting fosters a sense of community and connection among quilters.

Defining Couch Quilting: Couch quilting is a popular form of quilting that allows individuals to create beautiful and intricate quilt designs from the comfort of their own homes. It is a versatile and accessible craft that can be enjoyed by people of all ages and skill levels.

The process of couch quilting involves using a sewing machine or hand stitching to attach fabric pieces together to create a quilt top. This quilt top is then layered with batting and a backing fabric, and the layers are secured together through a process called quilting. Quilting can be done by hand or by machine, and it involves stitching through all layers of the quilt to create a decorative pattern or design.

One of the main advantages of couch quilting is its convenience. Unlike traditional quilting, which often requires a dedicated sewing space and large quilting frame, couch quilting can be done on a regular sewing machine or even by hand. This means that individuals can work on their quilts whenever and wherever they choose, whether it's in front of the TV, on a road trip, or during a lunch break at work.

Couch quilting also offers a wide range of creative possibilities. Quilters can experiment with different fabric combinations, colors, and patterns to create unique and personalized designs. They can also incorporate various quilting techniques, such as appliqué, patchwork, or embroidery, to add texture and visual interest to their quilts. The flexibility of couch quilting allows quilters to express their creativity and make quilts that reflect their individual style and preferences.

In addition to being a creative outlet, couch quilting also offers numerous benefits for the quilter. It can be a relaxing and therapeutic activity, providing a sense of calm and mindfulness. The repetitive nature of stitching can help reduce stress and anxiety, and the focus required to create intricate quilt designs can help improve concentration and mental clarity.

Couch quilting also fosters a sense of accomplishment and pride. Completing a quilt, whether it's a small wall hanging or a large bedspread, is a tangible and lasting achievement. Quilters can showcase their finished quilts in their homes or give them as thoughtful and meaningful gifts to loved ones.

Furthermore, couch quilting is a social activity that can bring people together. Quilters often join quilting groups or attend quilting retreats and workshops to connect with others who share their passion for quilting. These gatherings provide opportunities for learning, sharing ideas, and building friendships with fellow quilters.

The Appeal and Advantages of Couch Quilting: Couch quilting is a popular and enjoyable activity that has gained a lot of appeal in recent years. It involves creating beautiful and intricate quilt designs while comfortably sitting on your couch. This form of quilting offers numerous advantages that make it a preferred choice for many quilting enthusiasts.

One of the main appeals of couch quilting is the convenience it offers. Unlike traditional quilting methods that require a dedicated workspace and a large quilting frame, couch quilting can be done anywhere in your home. All you need is a comfortable couch, a quilting hoop or frame, and your quilting supplies. This flexibility allows you to quilt while watching TV, spending time with your family, or simply relaxing in the comfort of your own home.

Another advantage of couch quilting is the reduced physical strain it puts on your body. Traditional quilting often involves standing or sitting at a table for long periods of time, which can lead to back, neck, and shoulder pain. With couch quilting, you can sit in a comfortable position that supports your back and allows you to quilt for extended periods without discomfort. This makes it a great option for those with physical limitations or health conditions that make traditional quilting difficult.

Couch quilting also offers a wide range of design possibilities. With the use of quilting templates, stencils, and rulers, you can create intricate and detailed quilt patterns without the need for complex and time-consuming hand quilting techniques. This allows you to experiment with different designs and techniques, and easily incorporate them into your quilting projects. Additionally, couch quilting provides the opportunity to work on multiple projects simultaneously, as you can easily switch between them without the need to set up and take down a large quilting frame.

Furthermore, couch quilting is a great way to destress and relax. The repetitive and rhythmic motion of quilting can be soothing and therapeutic, helping to calm the mind and promote a sense of mindfulness. It allows you to focus on the present moment and engage in a creative activity that brings joy and satisfaction. Many quilters find that couch quilting provides a sense of accomplishment and fulfillment, as they see their quilt designs come to life.

In conclusion, couch quilting offers a convenient, comfortable, and enjoyable way to engage in the art of quilting. It provides numerous advantages, including convenience, reduced physical strain, design possibilities, and the opportunity for relaxation and stress relief. Whether you are a seasoned quilter or a beginner, couch quilting is

Comprehensive Guide to Selecting Materials of Couch Quilting:
The Comprehensive Guide to Selecting Materials for Couch Quilting is a detailed resource that aims to provide you with all the necessary information and guidance to make an informed decision when it comes to choosing the right materials for your couch quilting project. Whether you are a beginner or an experienced quilter, this guide will help you understand the various factors to consider and the different options available to you.

When it comes to couch quilting, the choice of materials plays a crucial role in determining the overall look, feel, and durability of the finished product. Therefore, it is important to carefully consider each aspect before making a final decision.

One of the first things to consider is the type of fabric you want to use for your couch quilting project. There are numerous options available, ranging from natural fibers like cotton and linen to synthetic materials like polyester and nylon. Each type of fabric has its own unique characteristics and advantages. For example, cotton is known for its softness and breathability, while polyester offers durability and resistance to wrinkles. It is important to choose a fabric that not only suits your personal preferences but also complements the overall aesthetic of your couch.

Another important factor to consider is the weight and thickness of the fabric. The weight of the fabric will determine how warm and cozy your quilt will be, while the thickness will affect the overall appearance and drape of the finished product. It is important to strike a balance between comfort and aesthetics when selecting the weight and thickness of the fabric.

In addition to the fabric, the choice of batting or filling material is equally important. Batting is the layer of material that provides insulation and loft to the quilt. There are various types of batting available, such as cotton, polyester, wool, and bamboo. Each type of batting has its own unique characteristics, such as warmth, breathability, and washability. It is important to choose a batting that suits your specific needs and preferences.

Furthermore, the thread used for quilting is another crucial consideration. The thread not only holds the layers of fabric and batting together but also adds decorative elements to the quilt. It is important to choose a thread that is strong, durable, and colorfast. Cotton and polyester threads are commonly used for quilting, as they offer strength and versatility.

Lastly, it is important to consider any additional embellishments or decorative elements you may want to incorporate into your couch quilting project. This could include appliques, embroidery, or even beadwork.

Essential Tools for Couch Quilting: Couch quilting is a popular and enjoyable hobby that allows individuals to create beautiful and functional quilts from the comfort of their own homes. While traditional quilting may require a dedicated sewing room or workspace, couch quilting offers the convenience of being able to work on projects while relaxing on the couch. However, in order to successfully engage in couch quilting, it is important to have the essential tools and supplies on hand.

One of the most important tools for couch quilting is a sewing machine. While hand quilting is certainly an option, a sewing machine can greatly speed up the quilting process and make it more efficient. When choosing a sewing machine for couch quilting, it is important to consider factors such as the machine's size, weight, and ease of use. Additionally, look for a machine that offers a variety of stitch options and adjustable speed settings to accommodate different quilting techniques.

In addition to a sewing machine, a cutting mat and rotary cutter are essential tools for couch quilting. These tools allow quilters to accurately and easily cut fabric into the desired shapes and sizes. A cutting mat provides a stable surface for cutting, while a rotary cutter offers precision and control. When selecting a cutting mat, look for one that is self-healing and has clear markings for accurate measurements. As for the rotary cutter, choose one with a comfortable grip and a sharp blade that can easily cut through multiple layers of fabric.

Another important tool for couch quilting is a quilting ruler. This tool is used to measure and mark fabric for cutting and piecing. A quilting ruler should be transparent, with clear markings for accurate measurements. Look for a ruler that offers a variety of shapes and sizes, such as squares, rectangles, and triangles, to accommodate different quilting patterns and designs.

Thread is another essential supply for couch quilting. Choose a high-quality thread that is strong and durable, as quilts are meant to be used and washed frequently. Consider using a thread that matches or complements the colors of your fabric to create a cohesive and visually appealing quilt.

Pins and needles are also important tools for couch quilting. Pins are used to hold fabric pieces together while sewing, while needles are used for hand quilting or for sewing on binding. Look for sharp, sturdy pins and needles that are specifically designed for quilting to ensure smooth and precise stitching.

Lastly, a comfortable and supportive chair or couch is essential for couch quilting.

Setting Up Your Quilting Space Comfortably of Couch Quilting: Setting up your quilting space comfortably is essential for a successful and enjoyable couch quilting experience. Whether you are a seasoned quilter or just starting out, having a dedicated space for your quilting projects can make a world of difference in terms of productivity and comfort.

First and foremost, consider the location of your quilting space. Ideally, you want to choose a spot in your home that is quiet and free from distractions. This will allow you to fully immerse yourself in your quilting projects without any interruptions. Additionally, try to find a space with good lighting, as this will help you see your work more clearly and prevent eye strain.

Next, think about the furniture you will be using for your quilting space. A comfortable couch or armchair is a great option, as it provides a cozy and supportive place to sit while you work on your quilts. Look for a couch or chair with good back support and ample cushioning to ensure that you can quilt for extended periods without discomfort.

In terms of organization, it's important to have all your quilting supplies easily accessible. Consider investing in storage solutions such as bins, baskets, or shelves to keep your fabric, thread, and other quilting tools neatly organized. This will not only save you time searching for supplies but also help maintain a clutter-free and efficient quilting space.

Another aspect to consider is the ergonomics of your quilting setup. It's important to have a comfortable and ergonomic posture while quilting to prevent strain or injury. Make sure your couch or chair is at the right height for your work surface, and consider using a quilting frame or hoop to hold your fabric in place, reducing the strain on your hands and wrists.

Additionally, don't forget about the importance of having a designated space for your sewing machine if you plan on using one for your quilting projects. Ensure that your sewing machine is set up on a sturdy table or desk at a comfortable height, with enough space for maneuvering your fabric. Having a dedicated sewing area will make it easier to switch between hand quilting and machine quilting, depending on your preferences and project requirements.

Lastly, don't forget to add personal touches to your quilting space to make it truly your own. Consider adding decorative elements such as artwork, plants, or inspirational quotes to create a welcoming and inspiring atmosphere. Having a space that reflects your personal style and creativity will make your quilting experience even more enjoyable.

Significance of Embroidery in Quilting: Embroidery plays a significant role in the art of quilting, adding depth, texture, and personalization to the final piece. It is a technique that involves stitching decorative designs onto fabric using various types of thread, creating intricate patterns and motifs that enhance the overall aesthetic appeal of the quilt.

One of the main reasons why embroidery is highly valued in quilting is its ability to bring a sense of individuality and uniqueness to each quilt. By incorporating embroidery, quilters can personalize their creations, adding their own personal touch and creating a one-of-a-kind piece. Whether it's stitching initials, names, or meaningful symbols, embroidery allows quilters to tell a story or convey a message through their work.

Furthermore, embroidery adds depth and dimension to the quilt, making it visually captivating. The use of different thread colors, textures, and stitch techniques can create a three-dimensional effect, making the quilt come alive. This can be particularly effective when embroidering floral or nature-inspired designs, as the intricate stitching can mimic the delicate details found in real flowers or foliage.

Embroidery also serves a practical purpose in quilting. It can be used to secure layers of fabric together, preventing shifting or bunching during the quilting process. This is especially important in quilts that are intended for everyday use, as the embroidery adds an extra layer of durability and stability to the overall structure of the quilt.

In addition to its aesthetic and practical benefits, embroidery in quilting also holds cultural and historical significance. Many traditional quilting patterns and designs incorporate embroidery as a way to preserve and honor cultural heritage. For example, certain quilting styles, such as Hawaiian quilting, are known for their intricate embroidery work that reflects the rich history and traditions of the Hawaiian people.

Embroidery in quilting also allows for artistic expression and experimentation. Quilters can explore different stitch techniques, thread types, and design elements to create unique and innovative quilts. This creative freedom allows quilters to push the boundaries of traditional quilting and create contemporary pieces that showcase their artistic vision.

In conclusion, embroidery plays a vital role in the art of quilting, adding beauty, personalization, and practicality to the final piece. Its ability to enhance the visual appeal, create depth, and convey meaning makes it an essential technique for quilters. Whether used for decorative purposes, structural support, or cultural preservation, embroidery in quilting is a versatile and valuable skill that continues to be cherished and celebrated in the quilting community.

Understanding Fabrics and Thread Count of Couch Quilting:

When it comes to couch quilting, understanding fabrics and thread count is essential for achieving the desired comfort, durability, and aesthetic appeal. The choice of fabric and the thread count can greatly impact the overall quality and longevity of the quilted couch.

Firstly, let's delve into the different types of fabrics commonly used in couch quilting. Cotton is a popular choice due to its softness, breathability, and versatility. It is a natural fiber that allows for good airflow, making it ideal for warmer climates. Cotton fabrics also come in a wide range of colors and patterns, allowing for endless design possibilities.

Another commonly used fabric is polyester. Polyester is a synthetic fiber known for its durability and resistance to wrinkles and fading. It is often blended with other fibers to enhance its properties. Polyester fabrics are easy to care for and can withstand heavy use, making them a practical choice for couch quilting.

For those seeking a luxurious feel, silk is an excellent option. Silk is a natural protein fiber known for its smoothness, luster, and hypoallergenic properties. It is a delicate fabric that requires special care, but its elegance and comfort make it worth the extra effort.

In addition to fabric selection, understanding thread count is crucial in couch quilting. Thread count refers to the number of threads per square inch of fabric. A higher thread count generally indicates a denser and more durable fabric. However, it is important to note that thread count alone does not determine the quality of a fabric. Other factors such as the type of thread used and the weaving technique also play a significant role.

When it comes to couch quilting, a thread count of 200 to 400 is considered standard and suitable for most applications. This range provides a good balance between comfort and durability. Higher thread counts, such as 600 or above, are often associated with luxury bedding and can offer a smoother and softer feel. However, they may also be more prone to pilling and require more delicate care.

It is worth mentioning that the choice of fabric and thread count should be tailored to individual preferences and needs. Factors such as climate, intended use, and personal comfort should be taken into consideration. For example, if you live in a hot and humid climate, a breathable fabric like cotton with a lower thread count may be more suitable.

Basic Hand Movements and Techniques of Couch Quilting: Couch quilting is a popular form of quilting that allows individuals to create beautiful and intricate designs without the need for a large quilting frame or machine. Instead, couch quilting utilizes basic hand movements and techniques to stitch together layers of fabric and create stunning quilted patterns.

One of the fundamental hand movements in couch quilting is the running stitch. This stitch is created by inserting the needle through the fabric and pulling it back up, creating a straight line of stitches. The running stitch is commonly used to secure the layers of fabric together before adding more intricate quilting designs.

Another important hand movement in couch quilting is the backstitch. This stitch is similar to the running stitch, but instead of creating a straight line of stitches, the needle is brought back through the previous stitch, creating a stronger and more secure seam. The backstitch is often used when quilting thicker fabrics or when creating decorative stitching patterns.

In addition to these basic hand movements, there are several techniques that can be used in couch quilting to create different effects and designs. One such technique is called stippling, which involves creating small, closely spaced stitches to create a textured and quilted appearance. Stippling is often used to fill in large areas of a quilt or to create a background for more intricate designs.

Another technique commonly used in couch quilting is called appliqué. Appliqué involves attaching smaller pieces of fabric to a larger piece to create a design or pattern. This can be done by hand stitching or by using fusible webbing to adhere the fabric pieces to the base fabric. Appliqué is a versatile technique that allows quilters to add intricate details and designs to their quilts.

Couch quilting also allows for the use of decorative stitches and embroidery to enhance the overall design of the quilt. These stitches can be used to create borders, add texture, or highlight specific areas of the quilt. Some popular decorative stitches used in couch quilting include the blanket stitch, the feather stitch, and the French knot.

Overall, couch quilting is a versatile and accessible form of quilting that allows individuals to create beautiful and intricate designs using basic hand movements and techniques. Whether you are a beginner or an experienced quilter, couch quilting offers endless possibilities for creativity and expression. So grab your needle and thread, and start stitching your way to a stunning quilted masterpiece!

Exploring Quilting as an Art Form of Couch Quilting:

Quilting has long been recognized as a traditional craft, with its roots dating back centuries. However, in recent years, quilting has also emerged as a popular art form, allowing individuals to express their creativity and artistic vision through fabric and thread. One particular style of quilting that has gained traction is couch quilting, which refers to the practice of quilting from the comfort of one's couch.

Couch quilting offers a unique and convenient way for individuals to engage in this art form. Traditionally, quilting required a dedicated space, such as a sewing room or a quilting studio, with a large quilting frame or machine. However, with couch quilting, all that is needed is a comfortable couch, a quilting hoop or frame, and a selection of fabrics and threads. This accessibility has made quilting more approachable for individuals who may not have the space or resources for a dedicated quilting setup.

One of the key advantages of couch quilting is the ability to work on projects at one's own pace and in the comfort of one's own home. Unlike traditional quilting, which often requires attending quilting classes or workshops, couch quilting allows individuals to learn and practice quilting techniques at their own convenience. This flexibility is particularly appealing for those with busy schedules or limited mobility, as it eliminates the need to travel or commit to specific class times.

Furthermore, couch quilting offers a sense of relaxation and mindfulness. The act of quilting, with its repetitive stitching and rhythmic movements, can be incredibly soothing and meditative. Many individuals find that quilting from their couch provides a sense of calm and tranquility, allowing them to unwind and de-stress after a long day. This therapeutic aspect of couch quilting has made it a popular hobby for individuals seeking a creative outlet and a way to promote mental well-being.

In addition to its accessibility and therapeutic benefits, couch quilting also allows for artistic expression and experimentation. Quilters can explore various design elements, such as color, pattern, and texture, to create unique and visually striking quilts. With the wide range of fabrics and threads available, quilters can mix and match different materials to achieve their desired aesthetic. Couch quilting also encourages quilters to think outside the box and push the boundaries of traditional quilting, resulting in innovative and contemporary quilt designs.

Narrative Quilting: Telling Stories Through Stitches of Couch Quilting: Narrative quilting, also known as storytelling quilting, is a unique and creative way of expressing stories and narratives through the art of stitching. It is a form of quilting that goes beyond the traditional purpose of creating warmth and comfort, and instead focuses on conveying a message or telling a story through the intricate patterns and designs stitched onto the fabric.

Couch quilting, as the name suggests, refers to the act of quilting while sitting on a couch or any comfortable seating arrangement. It is a popular pastime for many individuals who enjoy the therapeutic and relaxing nature of quilting. Couch quilting allows people to engage in a creative activity while also providing a sense of comfort and coziness.

When combined, narrative quilting and couch quilting create a powerful and meaningful way of storytelling. The process involves carefully selecting fabrics, colors, and patterns that represent different elements of the story being told. Each stitch is thoughtfully placed to create a cohesive and visually appealing design that conveys the narrative.

The stories told through narrative quilting can vary greatly, ranging from personal experiences and family histories to social and political commentaries. Quilters often draw inspiration from their own lives, memories, or the world around them to create unique and thought-provoking narratives. The stitches and patterns used in the quilt can symbolize emotions, events, or even specific characters within the story.

One of the most fascinating aspects of narrative quilting is the ability to incorporate various techniques and styles into the design. Quilters can experiment with different stitching methods, such as appliqué, embroidery, or patchwork, to add depth and texture to their quilts. This allows for a wide range of creative possibilities and ensures that each narrative quilt is truly one-of-a-kind.

In addition to the visual storytelling aspect, narrative quilting also holds a deeper meaning for many quilters. It can serve as a form of self-expression, allowing individuals to share their thoughts, feelings, and experiences in a tangible and artistic way. It can also be a means of preserving and honoring cultural traditions, as many quilts are created to celebrate and commemorate important events or milestones.

Furthermore, narrative quilting has the power to bring people together and foster a sense of community. Quilting circles and groups often form, where individuals can share their stories, techniques, and support one another in their creative endeavors. This sense of connection and camaraderie adds an additional layer of significance to the art of narrative quilting.

CHAPTER 1 - Introduction

>

    I have learned many quilting techniques over the years. There are so many quilt styles, that it has always remained interesting and exciting. I also love embroidery. This "quilting on the couch" technique that I have devised uses four different embroidery stitches. They are not difficult. It is a new style of quilting, and it can be done sitting on your comfy sofa!

No Sewing Machine Required

This quilting method does not require a sewing machine. When I was growing up, people sewed. You learned it from a relative, or from home economics class. My grandmother sewed all her family's clothing

These days things are different. Clothing is mass produced, and not every home has a sewing machine in it like they did in the old days. You don't have to have a sewing machine to make this quilt. Of course, if you want to use a machine to sew the 24 squares of fabric together, that is fine. However, I have included instructions about how to do this sewing by hand. The rest of the work on the quilt, aside from sewing the squares together, is hand embroidery. Nobody has to go out and buy a sewing machine to make this quilt.

This project is one that you can pick up and work on anytime you like. Once you get started, there is no preparation needed. It is like knitting or crocheting. You pick it up when there's time, and put it away till the next time. It is portable. You can take it with you anywhere you go. Everything you need can be stowed in a carrier bag. You could work on it on your lunch hour, or while the kids are napping.

Quilting is such a beautiful artform, that I believe there are lots of people who would still love to learn it. I have heard so many people say that it keeps them sane in a crazy world. It is very fulfilling work.

Some quilt techniques are difficult, and some are easy. There are some that look complicated, but in reality are quite simple. I was lucky with my early quilting, because I chose the log cabin quilt pattern. It is one that looks complicated, but is pretty simple. There are many types of quilting that would be frustrating and overwhelming to a beginner. This is not one of those. There are only four embroidery stitches involved in this technique and they aren't complicated.

One of the four stitches is used to sew the layers of fabric together. It is called spiderweb stitch. The other three stitches you will use to make the pretty and colorful embroidered designs surrounding each spiderweb stitch. These designs are embroidered only on the top layer of the quilt. They can be learned fairly easily, and they are fun. You don't need to go to any art classes to make these designs, they are more like doodling. I am sure many of you will begin to make up your own designs, once you get started.

You will be using your own creativity with each step of this technique. You will making your own decisions about colors and patterns throughout. That is the main thing I love about this style of quilting.

Quilting can become an expensive hobby, as many of us quilting enthusiasts know. I have written this book in such a way that the cost is kept fairly low. There is a full list of materials below, but it is not necessary, or even advisable to go out and buy all the items at once. Some of them will require some explanation, which will be included within each chapter. With each chapter, I will list just what you need for that portion. After all, one of the joys of quilting is the shopping. Who doesn't love to go to the fabric store, and it is more fun when you aren't breaking the bank.

Some of the supplies will be available at fabric stores, and some will be at craft stores or other places. I have noted the supplies that are not generally available at fabric stores, to make shopping easier.

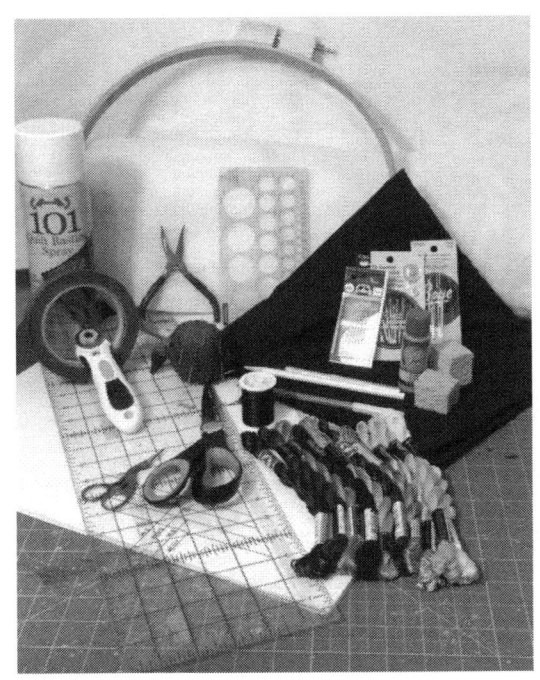

Full list of materials

1 3/4 yards of very dark, or very light fabric, either cotton, or cotton poly blend

Self healing fabric cutting mat

Rotary cutter

6" wide transparent fabric ruler

1 oz. bottle of matte fabric paint. If your fabric is light, use a dark paint shade. If your fabric is dark, use a very light paint shade

Sponges, the kind with the swiss cheesy holes, not the flat, manufactured ones

Quilting straight pins. They are longer than regular straight pins

Foam insulation sheet, optional (hardware store)

Pack of regular hand sewing needles

Two fabric markers, one dark, and one light

Thread to match fabric

Spray quilt basting

Scissors

A large piece of fabric for the bottom layer of the quilt sandwich. You should have enough left over after cutting the squares.

Iron and ironing board

Perle#5 cotton thread, as many skeins as you choose (craft or fabric store)

Pack of chenille sewing needles (any size)

Pack of #16 canvas needles

Embroidery hoop, approximately 12"

Scrap fabric to fit in embroidery hoop

Sheet of foam board, or corrugated cardboard (foam board is at the craft store)

Xacto knife

Circle template
Pincushion, optional
Heavy duty needle threader
Small pliers (craft store)
1" wide masking tape (hardware store)

CHAPTER 2 - Fabric Preparation, Cutting, and Painting

Supplies

1 3/4 yards of very dark, or very light fabric, either cotton, or cotton/poly blend.

Self healing fabric cutting mat

Rotary cutter

6" wide transparent fabric ruler

One 1 oz. bottle of matte fabric paint. If your fabric is light, use a dark paint color. If your fabric is dark, use a very light paint shade

Sponges, the kind with the swiss cheesy holes, not the flat manufactured ones (found at department or grocery stores)

Quilting straight pins, they are longer than regular straight pins

Foam insulation sheet, optional (from hardware store)

NOTE: The paint, sponges, and foam insulation sheet will not be necessary if you choose to make a whole cloth quilt. I will be explaining about this soon.

About the Fabric

For the fabric, choose a cotton or cotton polyester blend. Most fabric stores have a special area for quilting fabrics. Stay away from stretchy fabrics. They don't work for quilting and embroidering. Heavy fabrics are harder to embroider, and are not recommended for this project. One thing to look out for is that some of the cotton and cotton/poly fabrics do stretch a little, so just test them out while they are on the bolt at the fabric store. Very lightweight fabrics can be quite difficult to work with and could easily tear while embroidering. It is best to stick with cotton or cotton/poly blends.

I have chosen dark blue fabric for this project, but, of course you are free to choose any color you like. However, I would strongly suggest that you choose a a very dark or very light fabric. The reason for this is contrast. I have learned one important art concept that can make a quilt have a dramatic effect, and that is contrast. Meaning, light against dark, and dark against light. This will make your stitches pop with color. Otherwise, the embroidery can tend to fade into the background. It is much more fulfilling and exciting to have your colors stand out well rather than having them be more neutral looking. You should also remember this technique when choosing thread colors. Although the medium hues are more beautiful on their own, you lose alot of that beauty when putting them with other medium colors. Here are some examples:

Dark embroidery against light fabric. Good Contrast

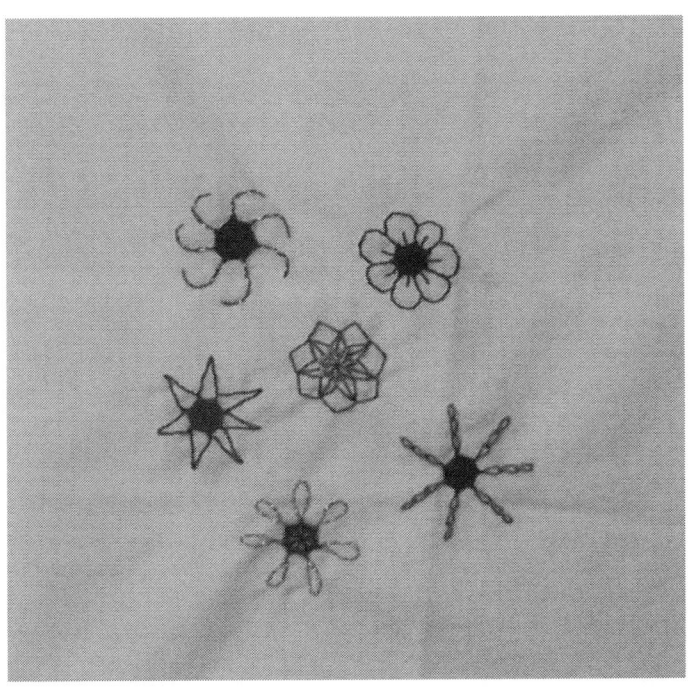

Light embroidery against dark fabric. Good contrast.

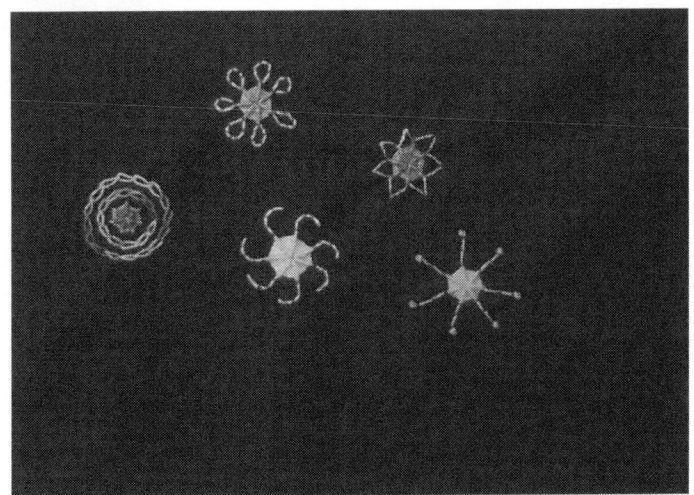

Medium fabric. Although the colors are pretty, they don't stand out well. Not good contrast.

Foam Board for Hanging Unfinished Quilt Pieces - Optional

A sheet of foam insulation board is a great place to hang and arrange your quilt block fabric pieces after cutting, however it is not absolutely necessary for this project. You can, of course, lay out the pieces anywhere that is workable for you. Foam insulation board can be bought in any hardware store. It is actually made to be used as insulation in the walls of houses, but it works well for our purposes.

Foam insulation board is lightweight and easy to carry, and is quite inexpensive. It usually costs about $10.00 per sheet. It comes in sheets that are 4'x 8'. You should take along some kind of knife when purchasing it, as it may not fit in your car, and you might have to cut it to a smaller sizes. It is basically foam, so it's easy to cut. For this project, a 3' x 4' piece should be a sufficient size to work with. If you have to cut it too small to get it in your car, it can be taped back together to make it big enough. I had to cut mine when I bought it, but I just used duct tape to put it back together. Of course if you want it bigger, that is up to you.

The board can be mounted on the wall, or put away somewhere when not in use. Some people cover the insulation board with fabric to make decorative bulletin boards. They are 1 1/2" thick, and much easier to hang things on than a bulletin board. You use your quilting straight pins to hold things on the board, and they go way farther into the board than tacks go into bulletin boards.

The foam board allows you to leave your pieces there until you get all the pieces arranged and sewn together. I used to lay my quilt pieces out on the floor while working on my quilt, and then put them away until the next time. It is much nicer using foam board. You can just walk away from it when you are done working, and then, come back to it later and start up just where you left off. For me it also has the benefit of not allowing my dogs to sit on them as I'm trying to lay out my arrangement. Don't ask me why they do this, but they all seem to like sitting on my quilt pieces.

Piecing and Quilting

There are two terms that need to be learned before we start, "piecing," and "quilting."

Piecing

Piecing is the process of sewing together blocks (or pieces) of fabric in order to make a quilt top. A quilt top is the top layer of three layers that will make up your quilt. The second layer is the fluffy stuff, called batting. The third layer is the fabric quilt back, made from another whole piece of fabric. When all three layers are put on top of each other, they are called a "quilt sandwich."

Quilting

Quilting is the process of sewing all three layers together. There are many many techniques of quilting, done both by hand and with a sewing machine. The kind of quilting we are doing here is hand work. It is custom, one-of-a-kind, and something to be proud of. Today's quilts are tomorrow's heirlooms. Once the three layers are sewn together, it is no longer a "quilt sandwich," it is a quilt.

Fabric Preparation

Before we begin piecing and quilting, we need to first prepare the fabric. The first thing to do when starting any quilt is to wash the fabric. The reason for washing the fabric before working with it is shrinkage. Some fabrics shrink when washed. It is especially important to first wash the fabric for this quilt. If you embroidered first, and then washed and had the fabric shrink, the embroidery would be loose. Not a good situation.

For this quilt, only washing is necessary, no drying. Let it air dry. Once the quilt is complete it should never be dried in the machine. Drying might rough up the stitches, or make the fabric further shrink. These stitches aren't real fragile, but I wouldn't recommend machine drying.

For future reference, for any quilt you ever make, wash and dry your fabric first. Even if you are not embroidering on it. Many quilts use more than one fabric, and fabrics can shrink at different rates. So wash first.

Skipping the Painting and Piecing and Making a Whole Cloth Quilt

The directions for the next sections will be concerned with cutting 6"x 6" quilt blocks, doing some painting on them, and then sewing them together by hand or with a sewing machine. If you like, there is another, simpler way to make a quilt that will allow you to skip the piecing and painting.

Not all quilts are made from piecing. Some are made from one single piece of fabric for the quilt top. These are called "whole cloth quilts." You can go to part 4 - "Making and Basting the Quilt Sandwich," if you choose to make a whole cloth quilt. However, if you have never used a rotary cutter and cutting mat, please read through the next section first. Instead of cutting the 24 6"x 6" pieces, just cut one large piece for your quilt top. If you would like to make it the same size as the pieced quilt, cut it to be 21" x 31", but it can really be any size you like.

Remember, for those who choose to make a whole cloth quilt, move on to part 4 "Making and Basting the Quilt Sandwich," after cutting out your single-piece quilt top.

Cutting with the Rotary Cutter

After the fabric has dried, we can begin cutting. You will be using your cutting mat, clear ruler, and rotary cutter for this. You will need twenty-four 6" x 6" blocks of fabric for this quilt top. It's a good idea to cut some extra blocks too. If you've never used a cutting mat and a rotary cutter, I guarantee you will love it. It makes your fabric cut like butter, and the pieces are precisely sized. Precision sizing of quilt blocks is very important. They will fit together easily and well. It would be very hard to accomplish these perfectly sized pieces with scissors.

NOTE: I have seen some pretty high prices in fabric stores for the mat, ruler, and rotary cutter, but have found more reasonable prices online.

Before cutting, fold the fabric in half, matching up the finished edges. If the raw cut ends don't match up (they rarely do), don't worry. We'll fix that later. Make sure the fabric lies flat when folded. Then fold it in half again, in the same direction. It is important to line up the finished edges and to have the fabric lie flat.

Folding is necessary because, otherwise, it wouldn't fit on the cutting mat. Lay the folded fabric on the cutting mat so that it lines up with the horizontal lines on the mat. Use the grid on your mat and clear ruler to make sure the cuts are square. The first cut is to take off the uneven raw ends.

Move the ruler so that the next cut will be a 6" wide strip. The lines on the clear ruler will show the correct measurements. Do this four times till you have four strips of fabric. Once all the strips are cut, unfold the strips, and turn them sideways. Lay them along the horizontal rules on the mat. Once again match the lines on the mat and ruler so that everything will be square, and cut the strips into 6" squares. You will need at least 24 squares, but it is best to have some extras.

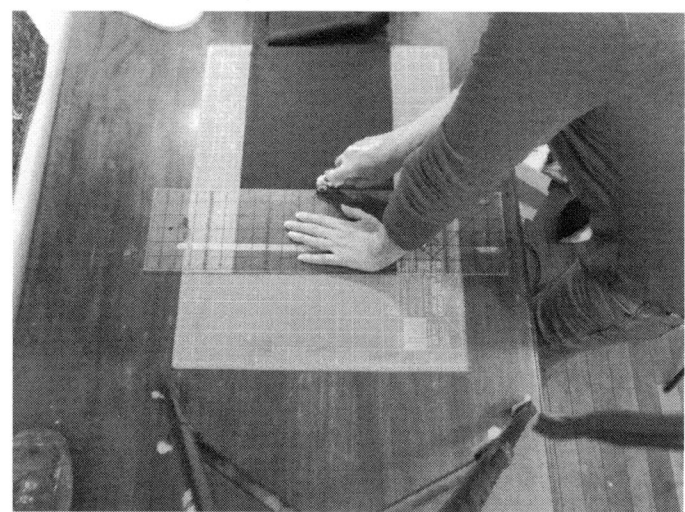

Fabric Painting

Next we will be doing some fabric painting. For this you need your sponges and paint. I suggest you do some practicing with this technique before you start on your squares. You can practice on either a heavy piece of paper, like construction paper, or some scraps of waste fabric. Cut your sponge into 1 1/2" squares before starting

I use paper plates as palettes for the paint, but any kind of heavy paper will do. Dip the sponge in the paint and stamp it around on a piece of paper or your palette, to get rid of excess paint. We don't want heavy, solid marks with our painting. You want to see the effects of the sponge surface. Then start painting on the practice material or paper. You want to end up with a graduated effect, so first go lightly over the whole area you want to cover. Then go over it more times, until you get the effect shown below.

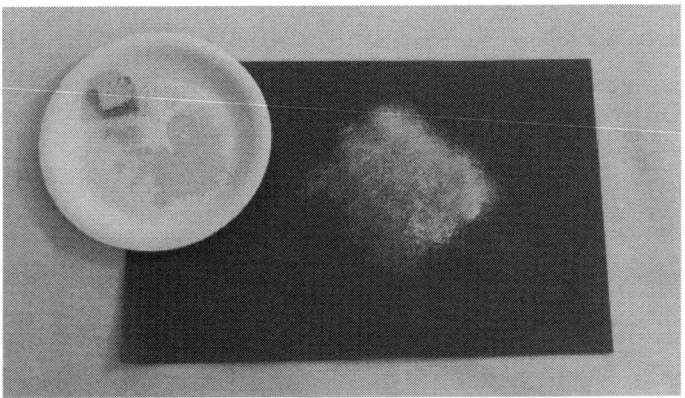

When you've practiced until you've become comfortable with it, you're ready to do the squares. They should be painted to make a pattern as shown here.

    Creating a graduated effect with paint (dark to light) makes a very dramatic look on your finished quilt. It's a simple technique that creates a very interesting and beautiful quilt top. Quilting that has no painting on it tends to look kind of flat. If you would like to get an idea of how paint looks on the surface of a quilt, I suggest checking out Laurel Burch's quilts online. She uses paint all over the surfaces of her quilts. It's pretty much a treat to look at her quilts.

    Using straight pins, hang the pieces up on the foam insulation board to let them dry for the amount of time the paint calls for. If you've covered the foam board with fabric to make it nice, then it would be best to dry them somewhere else, so as not to stain your bulletin board. Then arrange the pieces so that they create the pattern shown here. Now you are ready to start sewing.

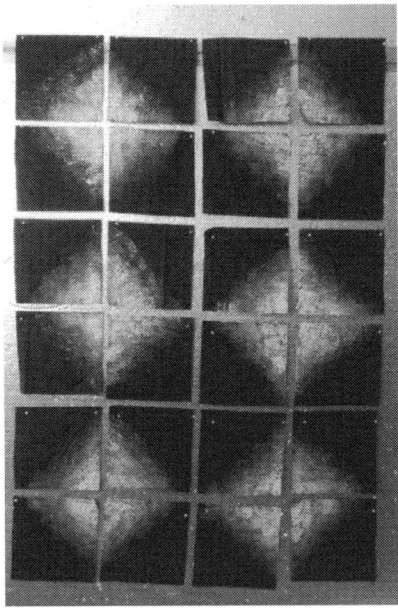

Please do not limit yourself to the configuration of the layout I have used here . If you find a layout that you like better, go for it

CHAPTER 3 - Sewing

Supplies

Pack of regular sewing needles

Fabric markers. You will need both a dark and a light marker eventually. Use whichever one works best on your fabric. I find that fabric pencils work the best for me, but there are other options to choose from.

Thread to match fabric

Iron and ironing board

Sewing

Now that you've got the pattern layed out, we can begin sewing. The first thing to do is to mark each square with your fabric marker 1/2" all the way around, on the back side of the fabric. This will create guidelines to sew along. You can skip this step if you are going to sew with a machine, as they always have their own measurements.

The next thing to learn in sewing is how to make a knot in the thread. Cut about a 36" piece of thread off of the spool, and thread it through the needle. We want to use a double thread for this project, so pull the ends until they are the same length. Next hold the ends between your thumb and forefinger with about 2" of the ends hanging beneath your fingers. Wrap the thread around your forefinger about four or five times. Wet the wrapped thread a little, then use your thumb to roll the wrapped thread off of your forefinger. Pinch the loop between your thumb and forefinger and pull the thread taut. There you have it. It might take a little practice, but you'll get the hang of it. Do not cut off the thread hanging beneath the knot, as the knot might come undone.

There are many videos online about thread knotting and hand sewing techniques, if you'd like more help in this area. In the videos they usually make rather large stitches, in order to make the demonstration clear, but you should make smaller stitches, about 3/8", to make your sewing stronger.

Now, we will sew the pieces together one row at a time, starting at the top left square. Take the first two pieces of the top row and pin them together with the right (front/painted) side facing together. Use straight pins to hold the pieces in place. Put the pins in at right angles to the sewing line. You don't want the pins to get in the way of your sewing. You will be sewing on the backside of the fabric, in order for the seams to be hidden once sewn. After pinning, open them out a little and hold them next to the pieces on the board to make sure you are sewing the correct edges together. Don't worry if you get it wrong a time or two. Every person who sews has to tear out a seam sometimes, no matter how long they've been at it. It just goes with the territory.

Pull the thread through the beginning of the line you've made on the seam. Sew small stitches across the line you've marked, taking a back stitch every few inches. A back stitch is where you go back to the beginning of the last stitch you made and make the stitch again, over the stitch that is already there. This makes the seam strong. You can take the pins out as you sew across the lines.

When you get to the end of each seam, you will need to make another knot. To do this, take a backstitch on your last stitch. Then insert the needle through that stitch, but don't pull the thread all the way through. Leave a loop. Put the needle through the loop and pull, making a knot.

After you get the first row finished, hang it back up on the board and leave it there. Start on the next row down. We will sew one row at a time, before putting the rows together.

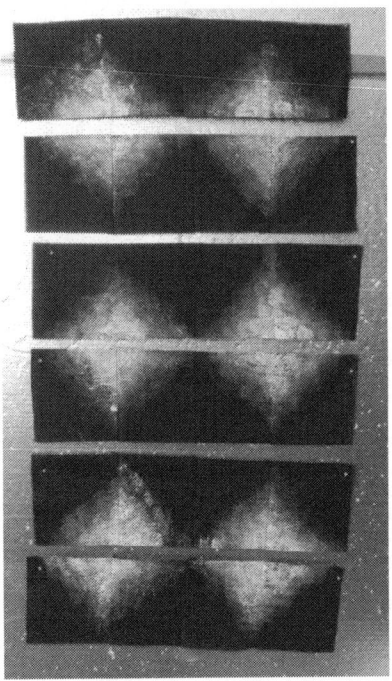

Before you begin to sew the rows together, take one row down at a time, turn it over, and iron the seams down flat. In normal sewing, you would iron the seams open, but not in quilting. Here, we iron both flaps down together. It creates a stronger bond. For these rows, iron the first row of seams to the left, and the next row to the right. Alternate this till they're all done. Then you can pin and sew the rows together.

When all the rows are sewn together, iron the new seams down too. They can all go the same way. I'm no fan of ironing, and avoid it whenever possible. But with sewing quilt pieces together, I always iron. Once you do it, you will see why. It gives the sewn piece a very professional looking finish that lays flat as you quilt. After doing it, whenever you see a garment or quilt that has not been ironed after being sewn, you will be able to tell the difference. It's a little bit of a hassle, but it's worth it.

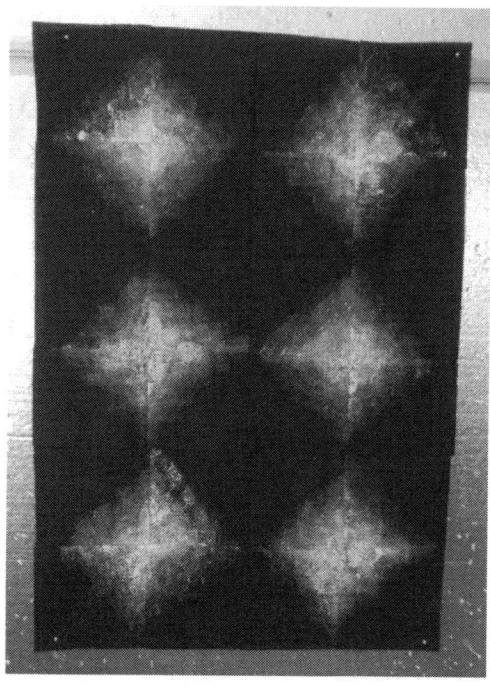

In this picture the quilt top looks a little unbalanced. The quilt is actually very straight and squared. The problem is actually my limited photography skills, so don't let this put you off, please.

CHAPTER 4 - Making and Basting the Quilt Sandwich

Supplies

Cotton batting

Spray quilt basting

Scissors

A large piece of fabric for the bottom layer of the quilt sandwich. You should have enough left over after cutting pieces for your quilt top.

Making the Quilt Sandwich

A quilt sandwich is the term for all three layers of the quilt placed on top of each other, the quilt top, the batting, and the backing fabric.

IMPORTANT NOTE: Always use cotton batting. Although polyester batting has more loft than the cotton, it can flatten out completely after washing. I have had this happen to a quilt, and have heard from others who have had the same experience. Not a good thing!

First, lay the batting out on a flat surface. Place the quilt top on top of the batting, and using scissors, cut the batting around the quilt top, making the batting about 2" larger on all sides. The cutting of the batting need not be exact. Just estimate about 2". The extra 2" will eventually be cut off, when the quilt is almost done.

Next lay out the fabric for the backing. This is the extra fabric left over from making the quilt top. Lay the quilt top and batting on top of the backing fabric. Once again, cut around the two top layers leaving about 2" on all sides. So, now you can see that each piece is bigger than the last, going from front to back.

Cutting off all that extra fabric is one of the last things we will do, after all the actual quilting is done. They are just excess fabric, but necessary for the quilting process.

The quilt sandwich shown here is how the whole cloth quilt sandwich will look. Of course, quilts that have been pieced and painted will look different.

Basting the Quilt Sandwich

Next we will baste the three pieces together. Basting is simply a way of holding all three pieces together, so that they will stay in place while we quilt it. If we didn't baste, the layers would slide around, causing problems. Spray quilt basting is a pretty new method of basting, and I love it. Spray quilt basting comes in an aerosol can, like spray paint.

You will want to do the spraying on a protective surface, so it doesn't get anywhere it shouldn't be. I generally do it out in my garage, but the directions don't require it to be done outside. First shake the can of batting, and holding the spray can about 12" above the fabric, cover each layer. Start with the backing. Spray it, and then apply the batting to it. If it's not flat the first time, you can pull the batting up, smooth everything out, and lay it down again. Then spray the back of the quilt top and lay it on the batting. Always spray the fabric rather than the batting, it sticks better.

Now you're done putting the layers together, and we can move on to learning the embroidery stitches.

CHAPTER 5 - Embroidery

List of supplies for this chapter

DMC perle #5 cotton thread, in as many colors as you want (fabric or craft store)

Pack of chenille sewing needles

Number 16 size canvass needles. These needles have a blunt tip, and may be plastic.

Embroidery hoop around 12" in size

Scrap fabric to fit in hoop

Foam board (craft store) or cardboard (the heavy, corrugated kind)

Xacto knife(fabric or craft store)

Circle template

Pincushion, optional

Heavy Duty Needle Threader

About the thread

Perle #5 cotton thread is not the same thing as the embroidery floss (thread) that is used in traditional embroidery. It is heavier and it is cotton, rather than rayon. You will generally find it in the fabric or crafts store in the same area as embroidery floss. There are two tags that go around each skein of the thread. The bottom tag will have a #5 on it, and a color number. That is how to tell that you are getting the perle #5 thread, rather than embroidery floss.

As I have suggested before, it is best to choose dark and light or bright threads, in order to achieve good contrast. You can choose as many or as few colors as you like.

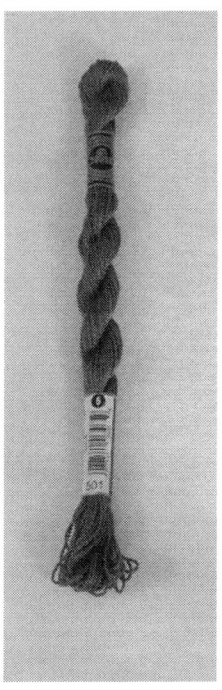

There are many colors to choose from, as well as variegated colors. Variegated colors mean that the thread fades into darker and lighter shades along it's length. If you wish to order variegated colors online, use the name "variations." That should help you to find them. Where I live, both the fabric store and the craft store carry perle #5 thread, but the craft store doesn't carry the variegated.

Before we begin the embroidery, there are some preparations necessary.

Making a Spindle to Hold the Thread

Before you can begin to use the thread, it must be wound around something, in order to keep it from tangling up. This is where the foam board or stiff cardboard comes in. If you use cardboard, make sure it is the corrugated kind made for shipping boxes. Foam board can be found at crafts stores. It is a sheet of paper-covered stiff foam, and is used in many art projects. You can cut it into cards to wrap your thread around. Although there are little cards commercially made for wrapping embroidery floss, they don't work for perle #5 thread. It is too heavy. So I figured a way to make my own.

In order to make the cards, use your ruler to mark the board into 3" x 4" squares. Use your xacto knife to cut out the squares. When cutting the squares, don't try to go all the way through the board on the first pass. It won't go. Just make several passes over the same line. This will make it easy.

Next cut some indentations into two opposite sides of the card, about 1/4" deep and 1" long. Then cut a couple of little slits into these two sides, about 3/8" deep. You can put the beginning and end of the thread through these slits, to hold them in place. As you get ready to wrap the thread onto the card, which is now a spindle, mark the color number onto the side of the card. When you start getting low on a particular color, you can refer to this number, and you know what to buy. When I go to buy thread, I just take these cards along with me.

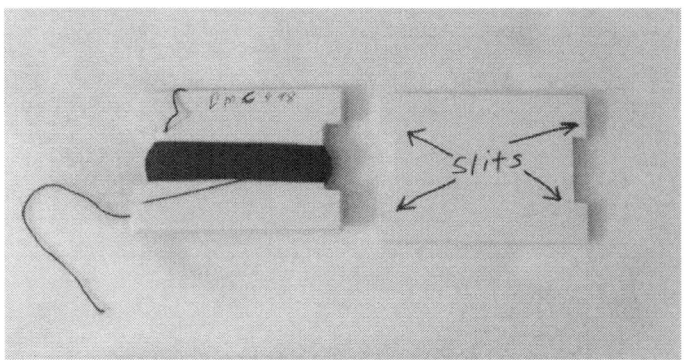

Testing for Colorfastness

It is best to test the strong and dark colors for colorfastness. Colorfastness means that the dye won't bleed when washing. To test the thread, take some of it, about a couple of feet long, and wrap it around your hand to make it into a loop. Put a little detergent on it, and run it through warm water to rinse. Lay it on a white paper towel and fold the towel over it to soak up some of the water. Let it dry. If there is no color bleeding onto the paper towel, then it is considered safe.

Although the colors are supposed to be colorfast, I have heard some terrible stories about thread bleeding onto fabric after washing. Especially red thread.

WARNING! If you order threads online, there is one thing to watch for. I have had the experience of ordering online and having the postage go up for each skein of thread. This can get expensive quick and is totally unnecessary. The thread weighs almost nothing. If you find this happening, find another online store. I have only had this experience with one shop.

Needle Threader

You will be using the chenille needles for this embroidery. The eyes of these needles are pretty big, but it is best to have a needle threader. The needle threader must be a heavy duty one. The kind for normal sewing, made with a filament to pull the thread through the needle doesn't hold up to this heavy thread. I found mine in the embroidery department of a fabric store. Perle 5 cotton thread is thicker than eye of the needle. If you don't have a needle threader, you will need to splay out the ends of the thread, wet it and smash it down with your fingers, in order to get it through the eye of the needle.

Practice Embroidery

Now that you have your thread prepared, we can begin to learn the four embroidery stitches. Before you start embroidering onto the actual quilt, it is best to do some practicing with a single piece of fabric and the embroidery hoop. It's a little more complicated once you start on the actual quilt, so it's good to get comfortable with the stitches first. You won't be using the hoop once you start on the actual quilt. You won't need it.

At this point I want to address the use of pincushions. The are not absolutely necessary to make this quilt, but they can be helpful. They are normally used for pins, but for quilting, I use them for needles. I keep my needles in pincushions because if I don't, I find that I loose them. They roll off the table and onto the floor and get lost. I don't want anyone stepping on the needles, or having the vacuum cleaner pick them up. Normally, with straight pins, you would push them straight into the pincushions, but with needles, you have to push them in and out. Needles don't have balls at the end of them, and can end up going all the way into the pincushion and getting lost.

Knotting the Thread

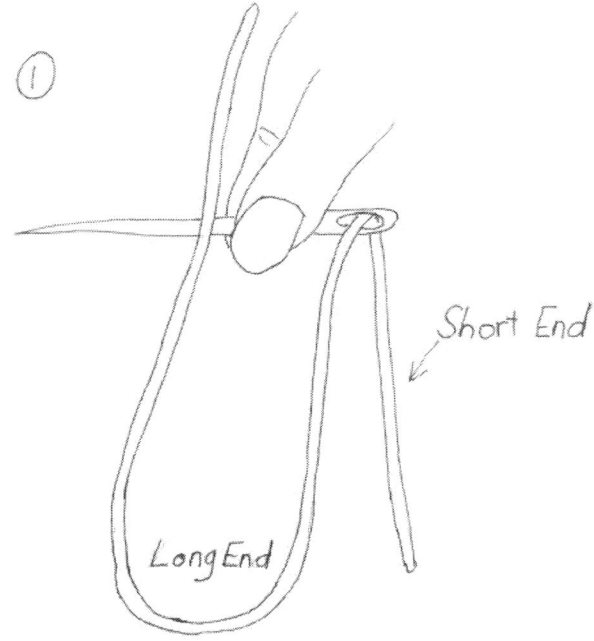

1. With the needle between thumb and forefinger, lay long end of thread over the needle, creating a long loop. In reality, the loop is much longer than is shown here.

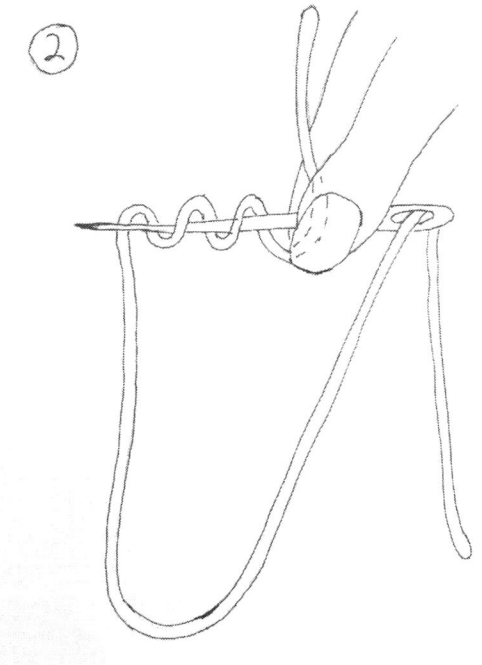

2. Push the thread along the needle until it's between the thumb and forefinger. The dashed lines show the part of the thread that is between the thumb and forefinger. Then wrap the thread three times around the needle.

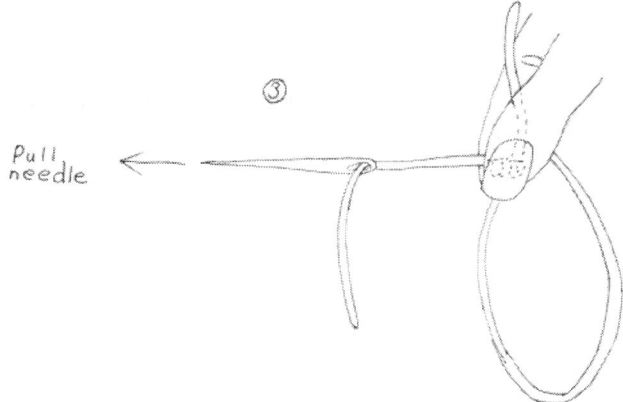

3. Push the three wrapped threads between the thumb and forefinger. This will create a knot (see dashed lines, again). Holding the knot firmly between the thumb and forefinger, pull the needle and thread until the large loop is gone and the knot is at the end of the thread.

This technique of threading the needle may take some getting used to, it did for me. But you will be using it so often, that soon it will be second nature.

The Stitches

We will be using only four embroidery stitches. They are straight stitch, chain stitch, french knot stitch, and spiderweb stitch. So let's start with the easiest one, straight stitch. Now is the time to get your embroidery hoop and load your scrap cloth into it so that we can begin practicing.

Straight Stitch

Straight stitch doesn't need much of an explanation, it's just a straight stitch. It goes like this.

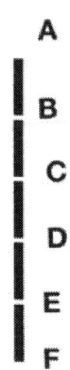

Come up at A

Go down at B

Come up at C

Go down at B

Come up at D

Go down at C

Come up at E

Go down at D

Come up at F

The stitch is about 3/8" long, normally, but can be longer when necessary. When you go around a tight curve, the stitches will need to be shorter. I'd say that about 5/8" is the longest you will want to go.

Chain Stitch.

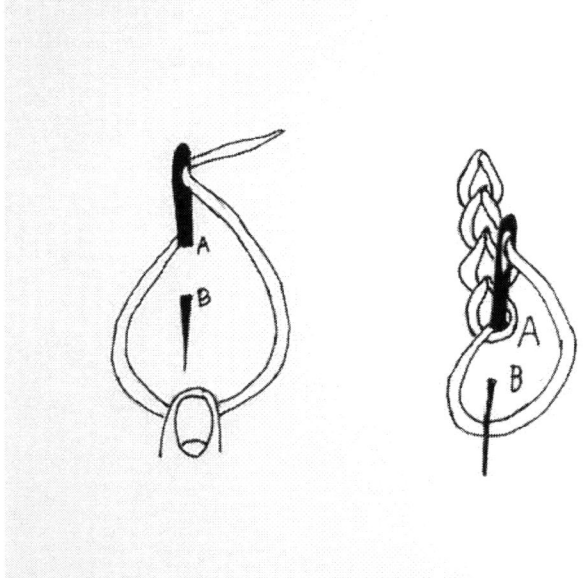

Bring needle up at A. Form a loop and put the needle down again through A. Do not bring the thread tight, leave a loop. Holding the loop with your finger, come up at B, below A, making sure the needle stays inside the loop. Maintaining the loop insert the thread back through B.

Repeat these steps, always inserting the needle exactly where the thread came out, inside the last loop - come up directly below, and draw through so chain stitches lie flat on material.

French Knot.

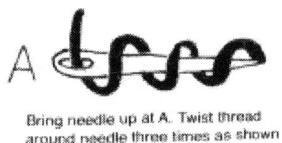
Bring needle up at A. Twist thread around needle three times as shown

Put needle back into A.
Pull the thread gently until it fits closely around the needle.
Pull the needle through

For french knot stitch, bring the needle up through the fabric, then wrap the thread around the needle 3 times. Put the needle right back through the same hole it came out of. Gently pull the thread so that it stays close to the needle and doesn't loosen up. It makes a nice little ball on the surface of the fabric.

We will only use french knot at the the end of this project. We will be making a colorful border of french knots all around the edge of the quilt.

This french knot varies from the original french knot stitch. The original has only one thread looped around it. But I wanted a bigger knot. So I added two more loops.

Spiderweb Stitch

Spiderweb is the stitch that will be the center of all the various designs that you will be making across the top of your quilt. It is also the stitch that will actually hold all the layers of the quilt sandwich together. But that comes later, when you are through practicing. Spiderweb may look complicated, but it is really quite simple.

This stitch begins with seven spokes in a circle, like a wagon wheel. The spokes go through all three layers of the quilt, and make a sort of simple star on the back of the quilt. The rest of the embroidery will be done only on the top layer of the quilt.

First, to create your spiderweb stitch, you will need your circle template. A circle template is just a flat piece of plastic that has cutouts of different sizes of circles.

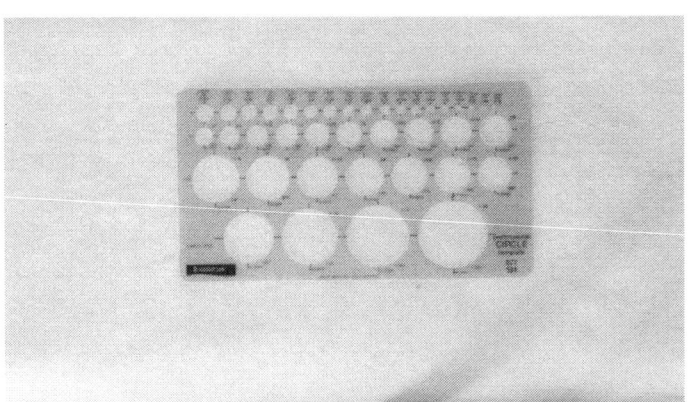

Each hole in the template is marked with it's size both in inches and metric measurements. We will be using the 7/8", or 22.23 mm size hole. Place the circle template on your fabric where you want it to be. You can even use some masking tape to hold it in place if you like. Masking tape works well for fabric because it leaves no trace of glue on the fabric once you are done with it.

You will not be drawing the circle onto the fabric. You will only be using the circle template as a guide to make some dots with your fabric marker.

You must ALWAYS begin the stitches in the middle of the quilt. It keeps the surrounding areas free for embroidering. It doesn't matter for now, as you practice with the scrap fabric and hoop, but later it will be very important to start in the middle of the quilt. As you make these spiderweb stitches, leave about four or five inches in between, in case you would later like to practice the design patterns around them.

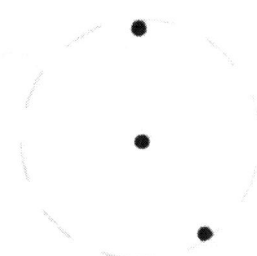

Place three dots inside the template, one in the center, one at the top, and one on the bottom, a little offset to the right

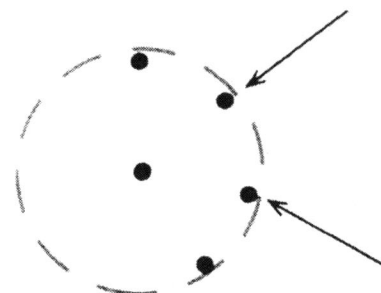

Add two more dots equidistant from the other dots, in the places shown by the arrows

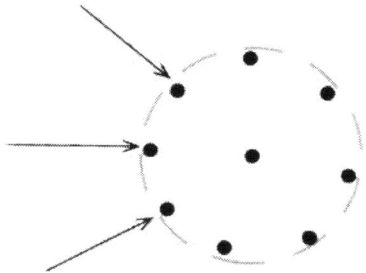

Add three more dots equidistant from the other dots, in the places shown by the arrows

Although we are using the 7/8" hole, you can make them a little bigger or smaller. The 7/8" size isn't a rule.

About the "equidistance," don't expect to have dots the perfect distance apart. It would be pretty hard to do this freehand. Mine are never perfect, but they look fine. So, don't worry about perfect dot placement.

Now comes the fun part. Pick a color from your collection of threads, and cut a long piece. Say around 50". We will always be using a single thread for this embroidery, so just knot one end. Knot it and bring it up at the center dot. Next pick an outer dot that is close to you and go down through this dot. This picking a close dot is not really necessary till you work on the quilt itself. But you'll see the importance when you actually start quilting. From there, keep bringing the needle up through the center and down through an outer dot, going around the circle, until there are no more dots. Now you have all of the seven spokes needed for this stitch.

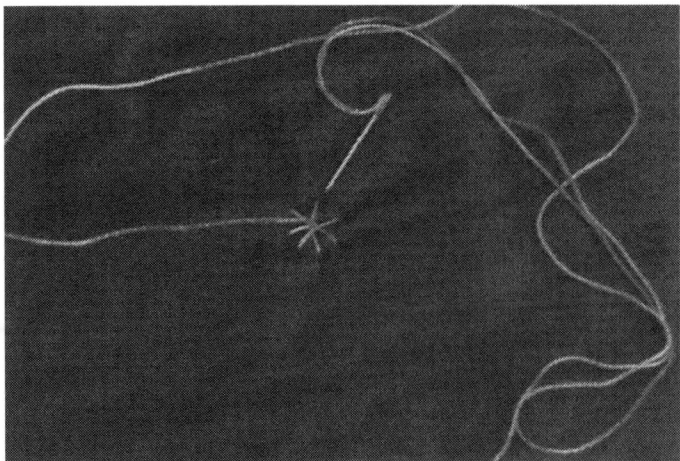

Now that all the spokes are made, and the thread has come up through the middle, we can begin to weave through the spokes and make the spiral. This is the reason for the long long thread.

Now is the time to change from the sharp needle to the blunt canvas needle. Sharp needles tend to get hung up on thread as you wrap the spokes. Blunt needles are so much faster.

Now we will start weaving thread around the spokes. You'll get the hang of it. Don't tighten the thread too much, just enough so that it lays flat. Slip the needle under a spoke nearest you. Then slip it again under the same spoke, but this time also slip it under the next spoke. Then go back under the second spoke again and also under the third spoke. Slip it again under the third spoke and also under the fourth spoke. Continue on around the spokes in this manner. You will be wrapping each spoke with thread.

Here is a view of the process of wrapping the spokes.

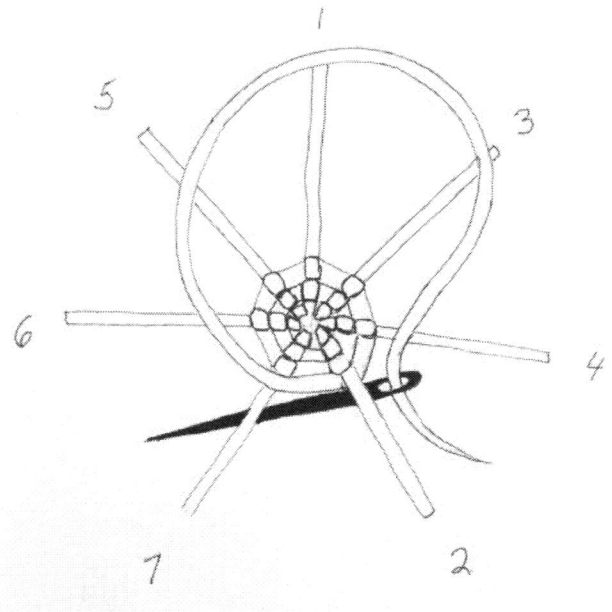

Once the spokes are wrapped, we will make a knot on the backside of the fabric. For the knot, go to the back of the fabric, and put the needle under any available stitch, leaving a loop. Put your hand through the loop and pull the straight thread through, but not the needle. This will make another loop. Pull to tighten. Put the needle through this new loop, and pull to make a knot. Now you have your spiderweb.

One thing to note here, don't worry if everything isn't perfect. If some spokes are filled and others not quite, you can stuff in another round or two, as long as it's not too tight and starts to bunch up. And sometimes, you can just leave a spoke end unfilled. This is supposed to be fun, not perfect. That's the way I do it. It comes out pretty, just the same.

If you would like to practice making the designs to go with the spiderweb stitches on your practice fabric, just read through the design instructions and pictures in the next chapter.

CHAPTER 6 - Quilting and Designing

Materials List
Small Pliers

Quilting

Once you feel comfortable with the stitches, it is time to begin the real quilt. It is also time to add the designs around the spiderweb that make this quilt so vibrant and special. This is where you begin to make all kinds of choices. You can choose any design style, thread color, and placement that you would like. Just make sure to keep working from the middle of the quilt, towards the edges, so that no part of the quilt gets blocked from sewing.

NOTE: I have listed pliers in the materials section. The reason for this is that it can be difficult to pull the needle through the heavily painted areas of the quilt top.

Quilting, as I explained earlier, is the part of the project that ties all of the layers of the quilt sandwich together. Usually this is done when all the work on the quilt top is finished. But this is a new way to quilt. We will be quilting as we go, using the spiderweb stitch as our method of quilting.

As you have seen, the spiderweb stitch has "spokes." It is these spokes that are our quilting mechanism. The spokes will go all the way through the three layers of the quilt sandwich. No other part of our embroidery will do this. The wrapping of the spokes and the creating of the various designs will be made only on the quilt top, immediately following the creation of the spiderweb stitch.

Here is a picture of how the back of the quilt looks after you have made your spiderweb stitches.

So get out your quilt sandwich and lets start quilting. Remember that you no longer need the embroidery hoop. You will work using only the 3-layer quilt sandwich. Pick your thread color, about 50" long again. Thread it and knot it. Then, using your circle template, make your dots to define where you want the design to be, on the top of the quilt. Remember, it needs to be somewhere in the middle of the quilt.

Now we will begin to do the thing that makes it possible to use embroidery do our quilting. We will be making our spiderweb stitch, but the important thing here is that we will be hiding the thread knots INSIDE the quilt layers.

Lift up only the top layer of the quilt just to where you drew your dots. Don't completely lift the whole top off, just lift the top layer till you can get to your dots. Leave the batting and backing basted together, and sitting on your lap. Now we will begin to make our spokes for the spiderweb stitch. Bring the needle up through the center dot of only the TOP LAYER of fabric. Then smooth the top layer back down onto the batting and backing. The spray batting will make it stick. This will hide your knot within the quilt layers.

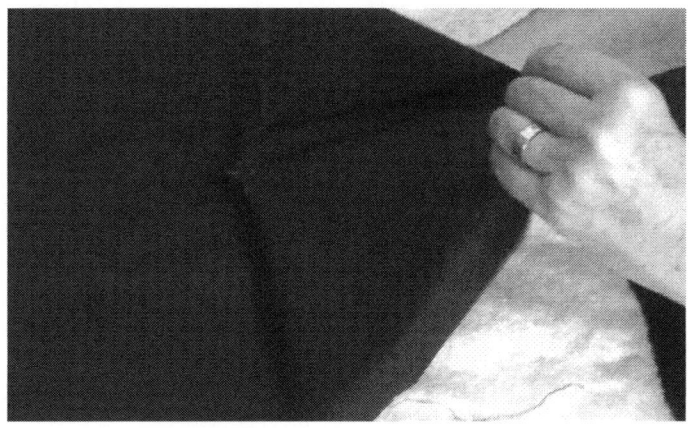

Now you make your spokes, GOING THROUGH ALL THREE LAYERS OF THE QUILT. Start with a dot near you. Put the needle straight down, through all three layers. Bring the needle up through the center dot. You may have to make a few attempts before you get the middle dot, since it is not marked on the back.

Put the needle down through the next dot, through all three layers. As you bring the needle up through the middle dot, check the back of the quilt to make sure the needle is entering the back side where the last stitch entered the center. This is to ensure that you will have a star shape on the back side, instead of a bunch of random straight stitches.

Continue going around the circle of dots in this way. Going down through all layers and coming up at the center through all layers, checking each time to make sure you are making a star on the back. This means making sure all the stitches meet in the center on the back of the quilt. When the last spoke is made, and the thread has come up through the center, you can begin wrapping the spokes. Remember to change to the blunt needle at this point.. When the spokes are done, lift the top layer again, put the needle down through the top layer only, and make your finishing knot inside the layers of the quilt.

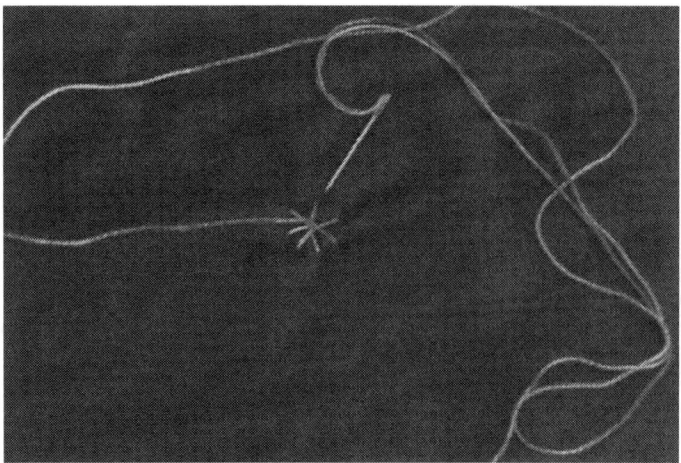

This pulling up of the top layer whenever you need to have a knot is the trick that makes it possible to use embroidery to make this quilt.

As you finish each individual spiderweb stitch, you will immediately surround it with one of the following designs.

Designs

Now comes the designing that make this quilt so vibrant and special. And it is also the part where you get to make all kinds of choices about color and design.

IMPORTANT: While working the design stitches, sew them to the top layer only. None of these stitches go through to the back of the quilt. We sew the stitches on the top of the quilt, and hide the knots inside the quilt.

Before I show the stitches, I would like to point out a helpful bit of information about drawing them. As you draw, for many of the stitches, it is a good thing to think of the stitches as coming from the middle point of the spiderweb stitch. It keeps your lines from looking choppy.

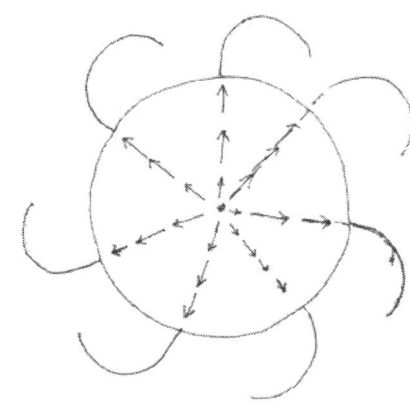

For some designs it's best to remember to draw as though you are coming straight from the center

Stitching Designs on the Top Fabric Layer

Choose a thread color, and cut it to about 50" again. Knot the thread. As you begin the design stitches, you will hide your knots, as you did when you began and ended the spiderweb stitch. Pull the top layer of fabric up to the spiderweb stitch you just finished making. Pull your threaded needle up from underneath the top fabric layer, to start the stitching, in whatever location is necessary for the design you will be choosing. Smooth the fabric down again, to begin stitching. You will be making your design stitches only on the TOP LAYER OF FABRIC. This is easy to do, and you won't need to raise up the top layer of fabric again until you are ready to make a finishing knot.

Now I will show a picture of each of the designs, and some explanation, if necessary. Although, these designs are really pretty simple. If you would like to practice drawing the designs, you can do this on your practice fabric, or on paper. As far as using markers to draw your designs onto the quilt, sometimes you will find it necessary, and sometimes you won't. That part is up to you. At first you may need to do it a lot, and then later, maybe less. I still mark some and some others not.

Small Star Design

Small star design is made with just the spiderweb and straight stitches. It is pretty straightforward. Just a circle of triangles connected to the ends of the spokes, and then a single straight stitch in each triangle.

Medallion Design

Medallion design starts out like small star design, without the lines inside the triangles. Then, taking it one step further adds more triangle shaped stitches all around, coming from the points of the first triangles. I like this one, because it looks fairly complicated, when it's really simple.

Big Star Design

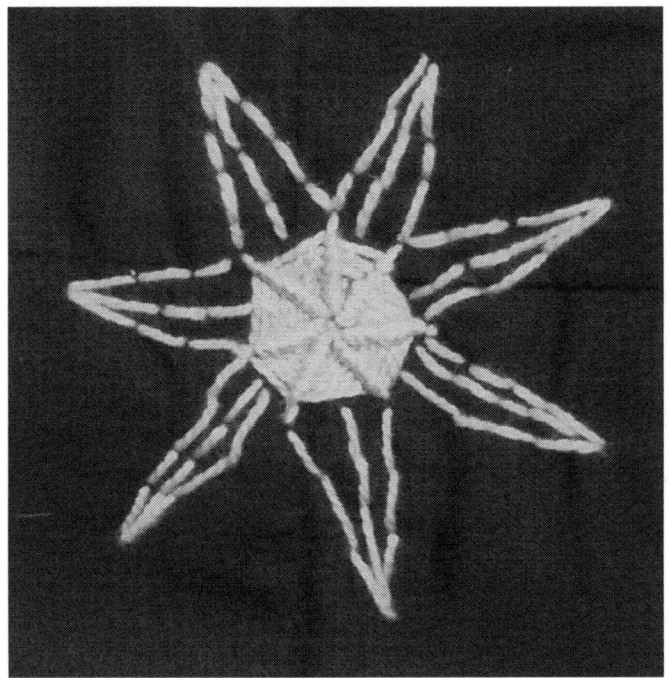

Big star design is pretty much the same as little star, except the triangles are elongated, and you need more stitches to make them.

Spiral Design

Spiral is a good one for practicing the "coming from the center," technique. As you make the straight stitches, don't immediately start the turn. Come out straight from the center a little at first and then gently make the turns. Also, remember, the tighter the turn, the smaller the stitches.

Moonlight Design

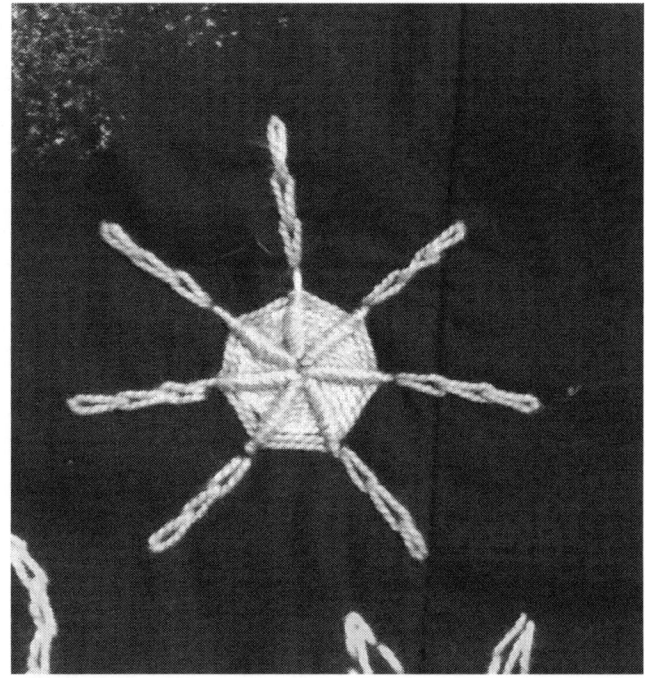

Moonlight design is just the spiderweb, with chain stitches coming straight out from each of the spokes. I make the row of chain stitches just a little longer than an inch, but, really the choice is yours.

Sunlight Design

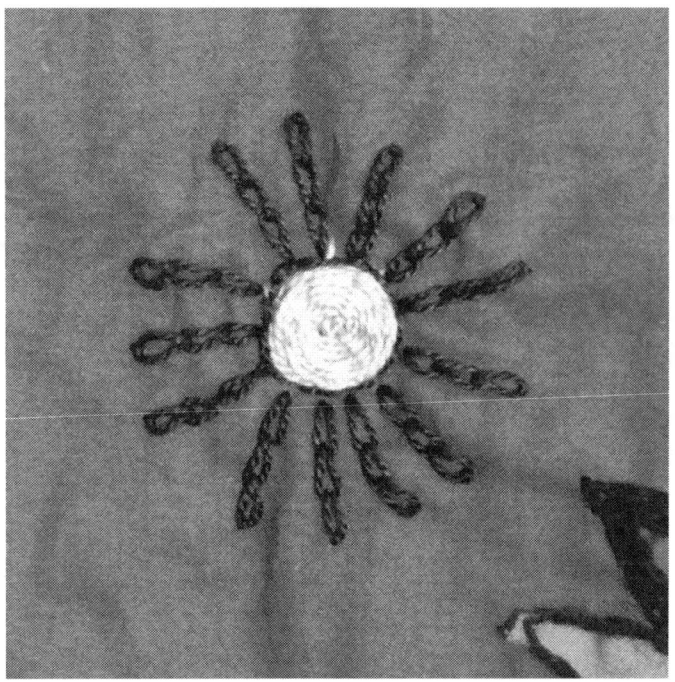

Sunlight design is just the same as moonlight design with more rows of chain stitches. Make the chain stitches coming from the end of the spokes, and then make another set of chain stitch rows in between the first ones. Remember, stitch as if coming from the center point. Although it is kind of hard to see the ends of the spokes in the picture, it is very easy when looking at the actual spiderweb.

Circlet Design

Circlet is just a row or two of chain stitches going around the spiderweb. I still always find it necessary to mark this one with fabric marker.

Petunia Design

This flower design is made with spiderweb and straight stitches. When beginning the flower petals, I draw a little line at each spoke, coming straight out from the middle of the spiderweb, and then, after drawing these lines, I draw the arc that joins each one. Then I add the little straight stitch inside each petal.

Double Petunia

In double petunia, you can see that I've made two rows of stitches around the outside edge. Drawing double stitches, side by side, can be done on any design you that you like, and it can add alot to the beauty of the design. As you can see, I have chosen to put two little stitches inside each petal.

Teardrop Flower Design

Teardrop flower is made of the spiderweb and straight stitches, and the petals are shaped like teardrops.

And that's it for the designs, although I'm sure many people will enjoy coming up with their own. I think that the possibilities are endless. Although the designs are simple, the resulting quilt is quite beautiful.

CHAPTER 7 - Finishing Off

Materials List

1" masking tape

Cutting down the edges

We are just about done now. The next step is to cut all the edges of the quit to match the top in size. To do this, just lay the quilt down flat, and cut the batting and backing layers to match the size of the top. Use the top layer as a guide to cutting.

Making a Border of French Knots

Quilts often have borders around them, usually made of fabric. This quilt will have a border also, but it will be made of embroidery stitches.

For the border, we will be making french knot stitches all around the edge of the quilt. Instead of using marker pens or pencils to show where to make the stitches, we will be using 1" masking tape as a guide. The french knots will be 1" away from the edge of the fabric and 1/2" apart from each other. Simply place the masking tape along the edge of the fabric in the area you are working on. Then make the french knot stitches 1/2" inch apart, on the top layer of fabric. Hide your knots inside the quilt. Now take the tape off and move to the next area to work on. Tape and stitch again. You don't have to tape the whole perimeter at once.

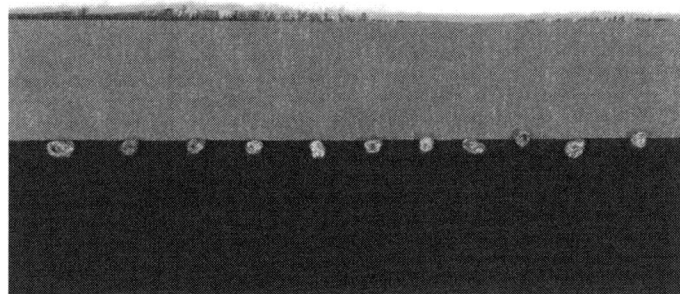

To make this border colorful, I just load my needle with whatever color I want, and then make the stitches till the thread in my needle runs out. Then I pick another color thread and use it till it runs out. I keep changing thread colors all around the border.

Finishing the Edges

Now we need to make the batting smaller than the top and bottom layers. Holding the layers of fabric away from the batting, cut 1/2" off of the batting all the way around. Now fold the one layer of fabric 1/2" inward, covering the edge of the batting. Fold in the other layer to match the first, pinning the two layers together as you go. When pinning, do not pin going along with the edge, pin it at right angles to the edge. Now slip stitch all around, to hold the edges together. This finishes the quilt.

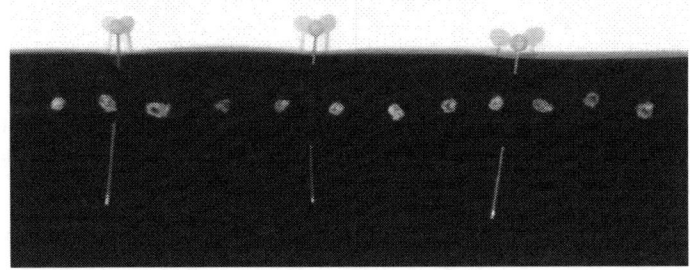

Slip Stitch

Slip stitching is done with regular sewing thread and needle. A single thread is fine. After making your knot in the thread, come out of the fabric through one of the folds, making sure the knot is hidden inside the fold. Then you make normal hand stitches, except you alternate the stitches between the top and bottom fold edges, to hold the layers together. One stitch up, one stitch down, and on like this all the way around.

When you get to the end, make a knot. You will not be able to hide this knot, but you can hide the thread end that comes from the knot. After you make the knot, put the threaded needle inside the layers, right next to the knot. Go about an inch inside the quilt, and bring the needle back out through the fabric. Cut the thread at the surface of the fabric.

Now we are almost done. Just one more thing.

Last of All

It is common practice to make a four inch "sleeve" on the top of the back of the quilt. A sleeve is simply a piece of fabric that you sew onto the back of the quilt, right at the top. You leave the sides of this sleeve open, in order to insert a rod to hang the quilt from. Dowel rods can be used for this. Small curtain rods also make nice holders for quilts. To make this sleeve, just cut a five inch strip of fabric, that is a few inches longer than the width of the quilt. Hold the strip up to the back of the quilt and cut the ends down so that they are 1/2" wider than the quilt. Set up your iron and ironing board. Place the 5" strip on the ironing board. Fold all the edges over 1/2" and iron them down as you go. Pin the sleeve to the top back of the quilt. Slip stitch the top and bottom of the sleeve to the top of the quilt.

And that's it, we're done.

I hope you have enjoyed this book, and this method of quilting. Happy couch quilting!

Manufactured by Amazon.ca
Bolton, ON

36912166R00055